M000198119

Life Calling

Life Calling

B.J.B. Phoenix

Published by Tablo

Table of Contents

Dedication

This book is dedicated to all the parents who need to be
reminded that they still have a life of their own.

And to all the young girls and boys who want to chase
their dreams with full awareness of the matrix of coexistence
that permeates this universe.

Gratitude

Thanks to my life partner, who has energetically explored
the depths of Life together with me, sometimes leading,
sometimes following.

And to all our children, who have always encouraged us
both to do whatever we truly enjoy, and taught us about Life
in their own unique ways. This book would not have been
possible without their amazing insights.

Beneficiary

All proceeds from this book will be used to directly fund the
education of girls who find themselves in under-privileged
circumstances.

Prelude

Most of the time, most of you do not answer My call. You just shrug it off as scam likely.

Most of the time, you don't even hear My ringtone; trust Me, my call is always loud and clear. Aah Jeeva! There's so much chatter going on in your heads all the time that cutting through it all is an impossible task. No matter, I just keep calling because that's My most significant preoccupation.

I am Life. The one and only Life Force infusing Myself into every physical manifestation imaginable. You have known Me since the moment you took your first breath. But do you really *know* Me?

Most of you take me for granted and go on with your daily routines as if I don't even exist. Frankly, most of the time I feel pretty ignored. Nevertheless, I don't have much else to do, so I constantly call every entity I inhabit in the hopes that someday, somewhere, someone will hear Me.

Every now and then, someone does. That's when We rise above the normal humdrum of existence and do some actual living. Otherwise, I just spend my time observing all the interesting activities the living beings engage in, the humans by far the most amazing and unpredictable.

You are probably wondering why on earth would I spend all my time just calling the beings I have already brought to life? Isn't everyone already 'living' if they are alive? Once I have brought them to life, isn't My job done? What more is there to talk about?

Those of you who have answered my call even once in your lifetime will require no explanation. But Jeeva! There are so few of you who have, which is why I feel the need to write this book.

One person who has always answered my call is Kaanja. He has been talking to me since he was five years old. His very first question to me when he responded was, "Will you still be there when I die?" Thus had begun his relationship with Me and, over the years, I have observed his level of awareness grow at a much faster pace than his physical years warranted. He is one of those who became a catalyst for the rest of his family to discover Me.

That's the only difference between those of you who answer My call, and those of you who don't; it's a difference between living and existing; a difference between conscious action and impulsive reaction; a difference between being alive and feeling alive.

This book is about how Kaanja and his family used Me to transform their existence. It is a story of an ordinary family living an ordinary life, discovering extraordinary fulfillment. I hope that through this book I can help you to do the same. There's no drama, no mystery, no drumrolls; just simple facts that you can test out for yourself in your own life.

Are *you* living, or just alive? Are *you* acting or reacting?

When was the last time *you* answered My call?

The characters in the illustrations in this book are not directly related to the characters in the story. The topics covered in the book can sometimes be overwhelming, so Ovi, Zak and/or Zim, or a poem shows up to provide some relief. Hopefully, they will also provide an opportunity to take a moment for reflection.

Whose Life is it Anyway!

Kaanja was furious. He was now eighteen years old. He knew exactly what he wanted to do with his life, and it was definitely not to follow in his father's footsteps. How many times did he have to repeat this statement before his father would accept it as reality?

"I don't *want* to build toys!" Kaanja appealed to his mother while she put the finishing touches on her chicken. "Why can't he understand that?" he howled pointing to his father, who was struggling to control his own temper. "I'm just not interested in taking over his business!"

"I've worked really hard to build this business!" his father yelled back. "And for whom? Your generation is so ungrateful. Your mother and I have sacrificed all our lives so that you and your sister can have a better life!"

His mother was wise enough not to interfere. She knew if she agreed with one, the other would be offended. She just pretended like her chicken needed her full attention.

"So why don't you let Kiara take it over?" Kaanja countered, trying to calm his voice and be reasonable. "You know what, she might actually be interested, and she will definitely do a better job than me."

"She is a girl," retorted his father. "This is not something she is going to be able to handle."

Kiara, Kaanja's twin sister, didn't miss a beat as she listened to the conversation. She continued to set the dinner table quietly; no one saw the blood rising to her head. She was in a culture where girls had a different set of rules to live by than boys. She had heard such insulting comments a hundred times from different folks, but the words didn't fail to pierce her heart every time.

Kaanja was keenly aware of his sister's presence in the room and decided he had had enough for the day. He stormed out of the kitchen, stomped up the stairs, and locked himself in his room with a bang.

As the common Life Force permeating them all, I decided it was time to make another call.

"Was that really necessary?" I asked Kaanja silently.

Kaanja sank in his bean bag chair with a big sigh. He was suddenly consumed by a sense of calmness; this is how I always knew that he was ready to answer My call.

"Where the heck were you when I was being so obnoxious?" he asked with a sense of remorse.

"Hello, excuse Me!" I replied, "I am always there where you are. I kept calling, but frankly felt pretty drowned out by the explosions in your head. You better get your head checked out after that."

"I really don't understand why it has to be like this," Kaanja continued, ignoring My complaint. "Is this *his* life story where I am in a supporting role? Or is this *my* life story where he is supposed to be playing the supporting role?"

"I belong to no one," I reminded him. "Or you can say I belong to everyone equally. Every being experiences Me as the center of their own universe. I don't need to tell you, Kaanja, that no life story is a solo act. As soon as I enter a physical apparatus, that entity is dependent on many other elements and beings for its survival."

"What do you mean?" Kaanja asked as if he didn't know the answer. This was always his way of finding his center of balance whenever he lost it, asking Me questions he already knew the answer to; which is just fine with Me, because as you can guess by looking around you, I love repeating Myself!

"This whole universe rests on a principle of mutual support," I told him for the umpteenth time. I know this is the one statement he always wants to be reminded of. "The level of inter-dependence at any point in time is a moving target for every living entity, and the balance is constantly shifting. So it is not a matter of either/or; it is a matter of continuously recalibrating the balance to see where the support is most required. What is irrefutable, though, is that solo act is unsustainable. You didn't get to this point in your own life story all by yourself, did you?"

Kaanja suddenly realized how hungry he was and ignored my question. "Let's go eat," he said, jumping up from the bean bag. "I will find a way to sort it out with Dad, but right now, we must eat. By the way, next time I behave like this, turn up the volume of your ring tone. Learn to be a bit more assertive, Dude!"

With that he tuned Me out and whistled his way back to the kitchen. That's Kaanja for you. He lets every moment drive his response to a situation. Sometimes it is with awareness, sometimes it is with what he later calls total stupidity, and sometimes he calls it highly emotional. But the thing with Kaanja is that he never dwells on his responses for too long. He has a way of bouncing back into the present moment at will and restart, flippantly unapologetic for his momentary response with a casual 'that's life,' but determinedly apologetic for his behavior when warranted. Someday I need to ask him why he thinks I should take the blame for his actions.

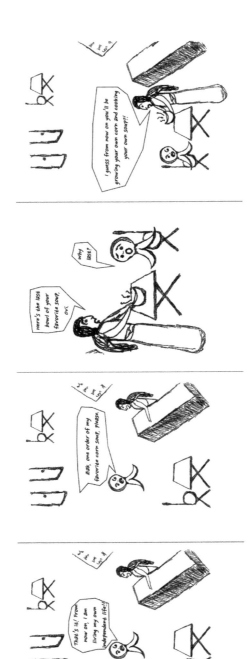

What the Life!

Kaanja's father watched his son storm out of the kitchen and sat down on the dining table with his head in his hands. He then looked up at this wife and said the classic husband words in a tired tone, "This is all your fault. You have given them too much freedom."

'What freedom?!' screamed Kiara in her own head as she put a plate in front of her father. Her mother knew better than to start an argument. She understood her husband's disappointment. His whole life had been a commitment to give his children a better life than he had himself.

"Why does life always have to be so difficult?" he muttered with a big sigh, then put his head back in his hands with a total sense of surrender.

"Hello, excuse Me," I tried to interject, "I am not difficult at all."

To my utter shock, for the first time since I have known him, I got a reaction from Kaanja's father!

"Who are you and what do you want?" he snapped, a little unsure but unable to ignore that he had heard Me. The irritation in his question was unmistakable, but it was enough for me that I had managed to get through. These are the moments I live for.

"It is not for me to want anything," I responded. "My job is only to give you the opportunity to do what *you* want."

"How can I ever get what I want when my own son won't cooperate with me," he sighed again.

"Hello, excuse Me. Did I say anything about *getting* what you want?" I asked rhetorically. "No, I said *to do* what you want."

"Oh, get out of here!" he snapped again, and then as suddenly as he had connected with me, he disconnected.

I did not mind. This was going to be the highlight of My day. That first connection is always the most difficult to achieve. Even a momentary connection is significant, because anyone tuned into Me at any point in time becomes grounded totally in the current moment. That is what I am all about, and that is why I get so excited when beings answer My call. These are the moments when the past falls off and the future flies away. Only the present remains. This is when *living* happens. It is almost like pressing the reboot button on what you call a computer (remarkable invention by the way!) and starting clean.

Most humans totally confuse My existence with the act of breathing. Of course, I enable breathing so that the physical apparatus I permeate can function. But I am Life. My purpose is to enable beings to *Live*! Living happens only in the moment. Reminiscing happens for the past. Worrying happens for the future. Living? That only happens *now*!

Kaanja's father looked up and saw Kiara bringing the food to the table. She is such a nice kid, he thought proudly. He looked at his wife and gave her an apologetic smile, once again genuinely appreciating the wisdom with which she had always handled her husband and children.

At that point, Kaanja returned to the kitchen and took his seat at the dinner table.

Kaanja's father looked at his family, looked at the delicious food waiting at the dinner table, and suddenly realized how blessed he was at that very moment.

He passed the rice bowl to Kaanja and said, "Tomorrow, let's find some time to discuss what exactly are your plans for your life. For now, let's just enjoy this scrumptious dinner your Mom has cooked up!"

There was suddenly a lot of crunching and munching in the air, but I saw no salad on the table. It took Me a while to realize that it was all coming from Kiara's head.

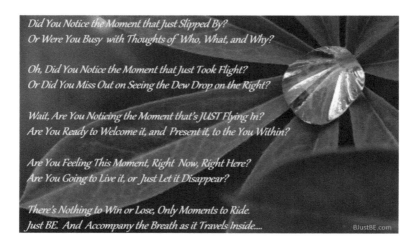

Did You Notice the Moment that Just Slipped By?
Or Were You Busy with Thoughts of Who, What, and Why?

Oh, Did You Notice the Moment that Just Took Flight?
Or Did You Miss Out on Seeing the Dew Drop on the Right?

Wait, Are You Noticing the Moment that's JUST Flying In?
Are You Ready to Welcome it, and Present it, to the You Within?

Are You Feeling This Moment, Right Now, Right Here?
Are You Going to Live it, or Just Let it Disappear?

There's Nothing to Win or Lose, Only Moments to Ride.
Just BE. And Accompany the Breath as it Travels Inside....

BJustBE.com

ARE YOU PRESENT?

Life Sucks!

Kiara ate her dinner quietly without paying any attention to the general banter at the table, although her mind was anything but quiet. Kaanja had apologized for his earlier behavior and told their father that he would really like it if they could discuss the issue rationally.

Other than some key disagreement points between her brother and their father, the two actually had a pretty good relationship with each other. And why not? Kaanja was a boy and their father had pinned a lot of hopes on him. And although her brother had a quick temper, he was generally quite mature and super aware for his age. He always found a way to deal with everything life threw his way.

(I must clarify here that I don't throw anything in anyone's way; all beings have the freedom to create the experiences they choose.)

Kiara knew that her father loved her a lot; that was not at all her issue with him. She just wished he would stop treating her like a little girl all the time. Why, why did she have to be a girl? And why was that a reason for her father, or for the whole world for that matter, to not take her seriously? It just wasn't fair!

Kiara had learnt to keep her emotions to herself. No one understood. Not even her friends. They were all happy to just wait for the time when they will find a husband and spend the rest of their lives taking care of their family. She sighed in despair. She didn't even know how to put into words what she felt most of the time. It was like a spirit trapped in a body, desperately trying to fly free.

From the time that she could remember, Kiara's most favorite moments in life had been her birthdays. Every birthday, her father would give her and Kaanja one of his newly invented toys. She was always given something 'appropriate' for girls. Growing up, she would often ask her mother about who had decided what was appropriate for whom? Since she never received a satisfactory response, at some point she had stopped asking.

Kaanja never showed any interest in the toys he got; he would always just give them to her. That expectation always doubled her excitement as she waited for each birthday. For several weeks after the birthday, Kiara would take apart the toys carefully and reassemble them back, always starting with the one that was 'appropriate' for her brother. After her tampering, sometimes, the toys would still work as intended, sometimes they wouldn't. Whenever she reassembled one successfully the first time around, she felt extremely proud of herself.

She never had the courage to tell her father that she would like to work with him; that she would like to see and learn what he did and how he did it. Her ambition had nothing to do with getting married and having a family. Her ambition was to invent new toys. She had so many great ideas that she wanted to put to the test.

Even though it was the twenty first century and women had moved gigantic steps forward in many parts of the world, almost every girl around Kiara seemed quite content to follow the local social norm that had been in place for centuries.

Not Kiara though; she was constantly fighting with someone or other in her own mind for her lack of freedom.

As she walked up the stairs to her room after dinner, Kiara was deep into a mental fight with her father for even suggesting that she would not be able to manage his business. By the time she got to her room, she had told him that she had had enough; she was going to leave home and take her chances out there. If she ended up dying in the streets, at least it would be by her own choice!

She threw herself on the bed in a state of total mental exhaustion, muttering angrily, "Life sucks!"

"Hello, excuse Me." I tried my best to cut through all the chaotic noise in her head. "How is this *My* fault?"

Everything suddenly went quiet. I couldn't believe it. Was I going to have two wins in the same day? In the same family?

"Can you tell me why I deserve to live a life like this?" she vented with full force. "Wishing every day that I would just die? What's the point of being alive if you can't even live your life the way you want?"

"What you do with your life is totally up to you," I said.

"But it's *not*," she screamed. "There are so many restrictions and expectations!"

"Of course, there are expectations," I said. "You also have expectations from others in your life, don't you? Your parents, for example? Everyone has expectations. So what?"

For a second, she seemed confused. She could sense a difference from the constant bantering that went on in her head all the time, where she played all the roles herself. She couldn't quite figure out who she was having a conversation with this time, but she didn't have the patience to figure it out, so she continued.

"I don't have the courage to go against those expectations," she said, suddenly listless, feeling the relief of accepting a truth she had never put into words before. "I can't tell my Dad that I want to make toys. I can't tell my Mom that

I don't agree with restrictions on how girls should behave. I can't even tell my friends how much I disagree with them on how they think we should live our lives. They all seem happy and content in their lives. There's probably something wrong with me that I cannot see things in the same light. I feel so small and insignificant. I feel so different. I feel like everyone else is better than me."

There, it was all out in the open now, figuratively speaking. She had always been so busy in her mind telling other people all the things they should not be doing, that she had never really focused on her own fears.

"What do you think others have that you don't?" I asked after a while, giving her time to absorb the full impact of her insight.

She thought for a long time. "Confidence," she said finally. "Everyone is so sure of their place in life; comfortably content in conformity; not afraid to speak their thoughts because they always know what the 'right' thing to say is."

"Who stops you from finding your own place in life?" I prompted. "Who stops you from speaking what *you* think is the right thing to say?"

Again, a long pause. Then she uttered softly, "Fear."

"Fear of what?"

"Fear of everyone thinking I am strange. That I am stupid. That I am just a trouble-maker."

"And what if they do think all that?" I asked. "Does that change who you *know* yourself to be?"

"....what.......if.....they......do.....think...all.......," Kiara mumbled sluggishly, and fell asleep.

Aah Jeeva! Story of my life. I spend so much of My time just keeping you alive while you sleep, eagerly awaiting your awakening.

LIFE MUST BE LIVED, NOT IMAGINED

Equal Life, Equal Rights

Kiara woke up in the morning with a sense of foreboding. She needed to make a presentation for her English finals. The thought of having to stand up in front of the class and speaking was terrifying her. She knew she would have to live through another episode of shaky hands, quivering voice, and excessive sweating.

She hated the feeling. She wondered if boys ever felt that way. It was not the topic itself; putting her ideas on paper was her strength. She always made sure that she knew what she was talking about, but the thought of standing in front of people and presenting was extremely nerve-wracking.

In her mind, she repeatedly played the scene when she would be standing in front of the class, with all eyes on her. She started to feel exhausted again as she absentmindedly worked through her morning routine.

"Why are you so nervous?" I asked, hoping we could continue our conversation from where we had left off yesterday.

She obviously didn't hear me. She was busy living her life in her mind as usual. From the time that I have known her, that's how it has been. If she were to live for another eighty years, she could spend the rest of her life narrating the life she had lived in her mind for the past eighteen.

Yesterday was a breakthrough, at least for Me. I wondered if it was going to be nothing more than a one-off accident.

"Why are you so nervous?" I persisted. Within a specific being, I really have nothing else to do. I just want to be *lived*. Lived fully, every moment. In real time. So, I just keep trying.

The corner of Kiara's nail ripped her stocking as she was putting it on, creating a big run. "Ugggghhh," she screamed in frustration, "Life sucks!"

"Heyyy!" I tried again, "Why is this *My* fault?"

She fell into her bean bag chair with a deep sigh and looked at the clock. She had gotten up early because of her anxiety, so she still had a good amount of time to get ready.

"Why do I get so nervous?" she asked helplessly. Somewhere amid her mental commotion, she must have heard Me.

"Why do you," I asked. "What are you scared of?"

She again had a moment of confusion as she tried to figure out who she was talking to in her head, then decided it wasn't important and continued her conversation.

"I feel like everyone is always judging me. Wrongly. I feel like I'm a nobody because I think differently from everyone else. I feel like everyone else is right and I am wrong because no one agrees with me."

"The presentation you have prepared, what do you think of it?" I tried to focus her mind on something concrete.

"It's a topic I know a lot about. I did my research. My idea is brilliant! I can explain my presentation with my eyes closed," she said with a surge of energy.

"Okay then," I said. "If you have prepared well, and practiced your speech, then you must present it with your eyes open. In *real* time. There is nothing else to do about it until the time of your presentation. Why are you living it a hundred times in your head when you actually need to live it only once at the right moment? What is the worst that can happen anyways?"

"What if they make fun of me? What if I forget what I have to say? What if the teacher thinks my idea is stupid?"

"Is there anything more you can do in this current moment to make the presentation better?"

"Not really," she responded thoughtfully. "I am actually proud of what I have put together!"

"Then that's all that matters," I said, "because that's all you can do. After that, it is what it is, and you just have to deal with it. But deal with it when it happens; not a hundred times over inside your head going through every possibility, because only one of them will eventually materialize. Focus your energy on what you need to do in your life *now*. Every moment of your life, deal with what you have to deal with in that moment. The rest will fall in place on its own."

"Easy for you to say," she quipped.

"If you are passionate about what you want out of life, then you must have the courage to speak your truth, no matter what the consequence. On the other hand, if you are ok to live your life in the sidelines only to please others, then it is also your choice. Don't blame anyone else for it. You have as much right to be here as anyone else, and as much freedom to make your choices in life as anyone else."

"I do?" she asked with a sense of surprise, and then wondered again who she was talking to.

"For sure. Think about who is stopping you?"

She did think for a long while, and then, "No one really. Just myself. I don't do anything because I think I already know what reaction I will get, and I always expect it to be negative. I guess I won't really know for sure unless I do things in reality instead of in my own head."

"Absolutely," I agreed. "And if you are convinced that what you are doing is the right choice for you, and it is not at the expense of anyone else, then there is nothing to fear. Others can react any which way they want, that is their choice. You have been living Me in your head all your life so it will obviously take some time to de-program. Patience is key. You must realize that others are not better than you because *they* think they are better than you. They are better than you only if *you* think they are better than you. That's quite easy to fix because it requires nothing more than thinking differently. In reality, no one is better nor worse than anyone else, I promise you that. I am exactly the same in every being. Everyone is just living Me differently in their own way, sometimes consciously, sometimes not so consciously."

Kiara had already moved on to thinking about whether it was too hot outside to wear a stocking anyways, and what hairstyle she would wear today. I could sense that she was making an effort to keep her mind on what needed to be done at the moment. I wondered how long it would last as I started to get slowly drowned out by a discussion on braids and curls, and whether it was time for another haircut. But I think you will agree that if a girl standing in front of a mirror is consumed with issues relating to her hair, then it is a good example of living the moment.

the sun, it's Truth to spread
warmth and light
yet constant explosion is its plight
the earth, its Truth to sustain
the living
yet it must endure the trodding & tilling
the tree, it's Truth to shelter and nourish
yet it must be trimmed
in order to flourish
we humans
so much suffering,
so much pain
yet the Truth we serve,
isn't it the same?
when you look deep within,
do you See what I See?
it is this Truth,
that can set us Free

DEEP WITHIN

Dear Life!

When Kiara came down for breakfast, Kaanja was already in the kitchen.

"Good morning! Where's Mom?" Kiara greeted him with a smile.

"She's not feeling well," Kaanja responded. "Nothing to worry. She just needs rest. Want some pancakes?"

"Sure," Kiara sat down on the table, determined to keep her focus in the present moment. For the first time, she actually noticed the beautiful tablecloth with a variety of colorful birds.

Kaanja brought two plates with pancakes and sat down next to her. He knew his twin sister would be stressed about the class presentation today.

"I wish we weren't in the same class. You are going to upstage me again with your presentation," he said, not totally in jest.

"Not really, but we'll see how it goes." Kiara took a bite of the pancake and savored the taste. She wondered if she had ever tasted pancakes before, or just ate them.

"These are delicious," she told Kaanja honestly, trying to stay calm and in the present. "There's nothing more I can add to my presentation, so it is what it is at this point."

Kaanja was a bit surprised at his sister's calmness. He looked at her suspiciously and asked, "What's up?"

Kiara smiled again. Kaanja had always been her best friend; she never had to tell him what she wanted or what she was feeling. He always seemed to just know.

"Nothing," she answered casually. She recalled the conversation she had with Me and struggled to remain centered in the present moment. Then decided it was too much and blurted, "I hate public speaking!"

"Well, you are not alone," Kaanja told her, "Three out of four people on this earth are on your side."

Kiara looked at him in surprise. "That can't be true," she said

"Just focus on friends," offered her brother. "Just look at me and make believe you are talking to me when you are doing the presentation. And look at Lucy and Cindy. They're your friends."

"Yeah," she responded with a hint of sarcasm, "And I also know that the Life Force that keeps me alive is the same Life Force that keeps everyone else alive. We all live it in our own way. No one has the right to judge another, because there's nothing that makes one superior or inferior to the other. I must just say what I have to say, and it doesn't matter if others agree or not." She stopped to take a breath, and then, "Yeah, it's all good in theory. Nothing works when I am standing up there with all those eyes on me!"

She was paraphrasing her conversation with Me, and already writing it all off as useless in her mind.

Kaanja just stared at his sister for a while, and then exclaimed, "Dear Life! Who have *you* been talking to?!"

"I don't know," Kiara said thoughtfully as she tried to figure out again who she had been talking to. She was surprised herself at the words that had come out of her mouth.

Kaanja was totally confused. His sister was acting weird. He simply shook his head and got up. "We're getting late for school. Let's go."

In school, when Kiara stood in front of the class, she once again tried to remind herself of the conversation she had with

Me in a desperate effort to calm her nerves. 'No-one sitting in front of me knows more about my topic,' she told herself. 'My perspective is as important as anyone else's,' she told herself. But she felt the shaking of her hands, the tremor in her voice, the sweat on her face.

Then she suddenly felt a surge of anger rising in her body. 'Equal life, my foot!' she cried in her head. 'I need to start taking control in my own hands,' she told herself with determination.

"As if it was ever in anyone else's hands," was My humble retort, which went totally unnoticed. I wonder if I will ever get used to being ignored.

She looked up at the class and said, "Speaking to an audience makes me very nervous, so I hope you will focus on my idea and not my voice." With that, she suddenly felt her nervous energy depleting as enthusiasm for her topic took over.

Even though Kiara had been unable to differentiate between the usual chatter in her head and her conversations with Me, I could see that she had for once consciously chosen to opt for courage instead of fear. She had taken a bold step for the first time in her life, and as we all know, every journey starts but with the first step.

Life is Now

Kaanja's mother lay in bed, with her heart hurting more than her head. Her family was reaching a critical stage in their co-existence, and she could see many important decisions coming up for every member in the family.

She had no meaningful complaints with her life. To the contrary, she felt very blessed. She used to answer My call often while she was growing up. After her marriage, it became more and more rare, and we haven't really spoken since she gave birth to Kaanja and Kiara.

Her husband was a decent and caring man according to her own assessment, and Kaanja and Kiara had turned out so well, despite all the things she always worried could go wrong. Her worrying was not unreasonable; I have witnessed this world becoming more and more complicated over the millennia, and the pressures on the younger generation have only continued to mount.

Still, Kaanja's mother had always taken her calamitous thoughts to an unusually unreasonable level. When her husband or the kids were out, she worried bad things might happen to them. When they were at home, she worried that she herself might do something that would end up in serious implications for them – like feeding them expired food by mistake.

Kaanja's mother was a generally aware and wise person. But for all her wisdom, she just couldn't shake this constant feeling of foreboding. On top of it all, she worried even more thinking that bad things will happen simply because she thought about them happening!

It was super stressful for her to live a life like this. It got in the way of her fully enjoying what was otherwise a fairly fulfilling life. She just couldn't get her mind to stop thinking about all the misfortunes that might befall her family.

After what had happened last night between her husband and her son, she was already seeing a full-fledged warfare between them and was fully expecting to lose her son for good.

"Why do I always imagine the worst!" she muttered in exasperation. "I am going to die of anxiety one day!"

"Hello, excuse Me," I tried to make an entry. "I never leave because of anxiety. In fact, that's when I make My most meaningful calls."

Her mind had already moved on to thinking about her daughter. She was not unaware of the strong resentment and rebellion that Kiara harbored inside. As a mother, she fully understood. She had very few regrets in life, but her most painful regret was about not having been able to support her daughter properly as she was growing up. She had allowed the social pressures to wear her down, and she knew it.

She recalled Kiara's constant questions about why different rules were applied to boys and girls; about who had decided that it shall be so; about what would happen if she didn't follow the rules. Kiara's mother would often explain to her that rules were made by the society they lived in, and it was important to follow them so that everyone in the society may live in peace. Kiara would always question who was society? Wasn't she a part of that society? As such, shouldn't she also have a say in what rules were being made? And was it right to make different rules for different people?

Kiara's mother was an educated woman, and well-aware of the important contribution women were making in so many other societies. She herself was quite content to be a homemaker; it was where she found a sense of fulfillment and that is why she had chosen this life for herself. Kiara was different. She had been seeing the rebellious spark in her daughter from the very early stages of Kiara's childhood. She regretted not having been more diligent in standing up for Kiara's rights. As she lay there thinking about it, she promised herself silently that that was going to change.

As a wife, though, she dreaded the storm that was brewing between her daughter and her husband. She lived the future story of their confrontation in her mind all the way to where she had already lost her daughter as well.

Her head started hurting to the point where she felt it might explode. "Dear Life," she cried, "why can't I stop thinking about all this made-up nonsense!"

"Hello," I tried again, "I am here, and you can. I have to say it gets morbidly scary in here sometimes, but most of the time it is pretty entertaining."

She stopped thinking only because the pain in her head was excruciating and overpowering. She had no choice but to be totally grounded in the present moment, her full attention on her throbbing head.

I seized the moment. "Take a deep breath and just relax."

She did. She relaxed her whole body and sank further into the bed.

"Notice the breath that is now travelling in," I said. "Feel it like a white light spreading all the way up to your head, healing every part that it touches." She was familiar with this drill because she had done it with Me several times while she was growing up. "Now notice the breath travelling out. Feel the pain leaving your body with it."

She followed my instructions only because she could do nothing else. She lived the present moment in all its discomfort; her attention focused on the only activity which required no effort from her: breathing.

"Aren't you tired of living such a stressful life?" I asked after a while.

"Oh, you have no idea," she sighed. It was almost like we had never stopped communicating.

"Oh, I do. Trust Me." It was good to reconnect. "How many 'bad' things have actually happened to you or your family so far," I questioned. I have no way of categorizing experiences as 'good' or 'bad.' They are simply events for Me. Humans, on the other hand, seem to have a way of rating them depending on how a given event makes them feel.

Kaanja's mother replayed her whole life from the beginning in fast-forward mode, forgetting her pain for a moment. "Actually, none," she offered when she was done thinking, surprised at her own response. "Even things that seemed bad at the moment weren't so bad in retrospect," she continued. "I can now see why they needed to happen. They became the catalysts that brought something good in our lives later or changed our perspective about life for the better."

"So, all your worrying turned out to be for naught in the end?"

"But bad things could have happened," she insisted. They happen to other people. They could have happened to us as well."

"Everything in life happens to move life along in the direction in which the life-holder desires," I offered my wisdom. "The caterpillar dies so that the transformation to a butterfly may take place. A country goes through a revolution so that undesirable practices may change. This whole existence is nothing more than energy in constant transformation; for something to be created, something must be destroyed because the amount of energy in the universe is a constant. Ultimately, there is no real gain, no real loss, just eternal experiences forever in transformation."

Kaanja's mother sighed again. "Yeah, yeah, the law of conservation. I know all that in my head," she lamented, "Science was my favorite subject in school. But I always become afraid when everything is fine, waiting for that transformation to the negative side. I just can't help myself!"

"Only *you* can help yourself," I said firmly. "No one else can. It's *your* life journey, others may be there to support, but only *you* must take the lead. Only *you* are responsible for the experiences you are having. It's all based on *your* actions, whether you took them knowingly or unknowingly. Only *you* have the power to change the course if you are not satisfied with the outcome."

"*How?*" she wailed, but suddenly became energetic at the possibility of finding a solution.

"Step one is to accept what is. It doesn't matter how you got here; what matters is that here you are. It is what it is, right here, right now. You took actions throughout your existence that got you here. There's no need to blame anyone, including yourself. There is no point in judging the choices that were made; just accept them. What is more important is to face the repercussions with equal acceptance as well. What is more important is to always ask the question 'where do I want to go from here?' There's nothing and no one that stops you from going where you want to go. Except you, yourself. It may be a longer road because of your detours, but every moment is an opportunity to consciously take that step in the desired direction."

She thought about what I had said for a long while, but said nothing, so I continued.

"Step two is to accept *fear* as a necessity. It keeps you from doing things that you know will result in undesirable implications. If you are afraid of death, you won't jump off a cliff because of fear; but if you are looking to die, you will. Fear is a choice. You choose what you want to be afraid of to protect yourself from going where you don't want to go. Different folks choose different things to be afraid of depending on their life purpose. But the bigger purpose of allowing any fear to be prominent in one's life is to create an opportunity to experience courage.

Step three, therefore, is to face the fear head-on. If it is a real thing, then do whatever you can possibly do to avert the danger. Focus on that instead of just worrying and not acting. And no, there is no reason why you cannot take an action. If you are afraid of another person, then you must find the courage to stand up for yourself, no matter what the implication, and no matter who that person is. If you choose to give someone else the right to have power over you, then there is no one else to blame."

I expected a full-on disagreement at this point because I know she had struggled tremendously trying to deal with her one cousin who had constantly bullied her when they were both in their teens. That's when we used to talk a lot, but she had never been able to muster up enough courage to stand up to her cousin.

"Do go on," was all she said.

"Once you have done whatever you feel is the right thing to do for your situation, you leave the rest to the Universe. If your worst fears do come true and the danger materializes, then that's the time for you to rise and just deal with it as best as you can. There's no need to deal with it a hundred times in your head before anything even happens. No matter how bad it may look at the time that it happens, someday, you will look back and realize why it had to happen. Trust Me, everything passes, and time heals all wounds. Sometimes it may take a long, long time, but heal it will; that's an irrefutable rule underpinning Life."

I paused again to let her absorb and then would have continued, but not surprisingly, before I could say anything more, she fell into a deep sleep. Aah Jeeva! This is how it always is. No one can take Me in my full potency for too long. Had Kaanja been here, he would have said to Me, "Learn to dispense in lesser doses, Dude!"

THE ULTIMATE TRUTH
HIDES DEEP INSIDE
YET LEAVES ITS TRACES
FAR AND WIDE
HYPERION TREE REACHING FOR THE SKY
CATERPILLAR TRANSFORMED
INTO A BUTTERFLY
THE BREATH THAT TRAVELS
IN AND OUT, IN AND OUT
OF ITS OWN VOLITION NUDGING
LIFE TO SPROUT

BJUSTBE.COM

HIDDEN YET VISIBLE

The Matrix of Life

Kaanja's mother woke up after two hours feeling unusually energized. Her head felt much better. She just lay there for a while observing her breathing, her mind totally blank.

"It's not that hard, is it?" I asked.

"What?" she asked.

"To just BE. And live every moment as it comes."

"Sure," she said without any emotion, "If you say so. But you were talking about managing fear."

"If your fear is not real, and just imagined tragedies that cripple you from enjoying life, then you just need to change your perspective," I continued as if she hadn't fallen asleep. "It's quite simple in a way. Whenever a thought of possible mishap comes to mind about anyone, follow it up by sending them your blessings. There's only one source of Energy that connects everyone and everything. You have the power to transform the energy. Replace your thoughts by thoughts of love, imagine them enveloped and protected by the shield of *your* Energy, which is the same as theirs. Especially a mother's energy, when selfless and pure, cannot be ignored even by the

Universe. Bless the people you are worried about, and then move on to focus on your own present moment.

What you must realize is that whatever happens to anyone is necessary for them to move their own life story along in the direction that they have chosen. It's their life story, not yours, and they have every right to make whatever choices they desire, and then face the repercussions.

However, knowing this does not absolve you from consciously deciding how you can support them. Just as they will face repercussions of the choices they make in leading their lives, you will face repercussions of choices you make in deciding to support or not.

Remember, ultimately, there is just One source Energy experiencing Itself in every facet possible, through a multitude of manifestations that play a finite role in an infinite Life story. Life and death are nothing more than a continuous transformation of this One source Energy. Life as you know it is not about a destination. The ultimate destination for every manifestation is the same: back to the beginning, which you call death. I am all about the journey. It doesn't matter how and when you die; it only matters how you live your life, because that is the only available window for experience. More so, the only guaranteed window is the present moment."

"But don't you need to prepare for the moments yet to come? If I spend all my money in the current moment, I may die in the next because I would have nothing to eat."

"Yes, indeed. If what needs to be done in the present moment is preparation for the future, then that's what you must do. But that's not the same as worrying about all the potential outcomes. Preparing is a constructive and energizing activity. Worrying eats up the current moment and changes nothing. Preparing is a concrete activity in real life. Worrying is living your life in your head while Life passes you by."

"I need to prepare for the next phase in my family's life," she said in a very neutral tone. "Time has come for Kaanja and Kiara to claim their independence. But I have to make them understand that independence doesn't mean breaking free from relationships. Inter-dependence defines the very core of our existence; survival, in fact."

"I see that you have not forgotten anything about the bigger picture," I observed, "although you have been spending a lot of your recent life walking a very narrow path. Indeed, just as no branch survives once disconnected from its roots, or no baby survives if left without a caretaker, no adult can survive without a support system around her or him. Solo act is not life-sustaining. Someone must plant the rice for someone else to be able to eat it."

She didn't know that Kaanja and I already had this conversation, but deep down she knew that Kaanja would easily grasp the depth of her message. He understood the interconnections of this physical existence, the important role that every single individual in every being's life plays to move that individual's life-story along in a way that aligns with her or his expectations from life. He knew that everyone plays the main role in their own life story, and a supporting role in everyone else's. He understood the intricacies of the complex, eternal matrix of Life.

Kaanja's mother had witnessed Kaanja's conviction that there was no problem on this Earth that could not be solved through adult and mature dialogue. He was convinced that eventually everyone was here to support co-existence in a manner that would fulfill each being's desire, and that communication was the wiring that connected everyone to everyone else.

"He just needs to learn how to keep his temper under control when having those conversations," Kaanja's mother mused.

Kiara was a totally different story. Her mother knew only too well the drama that was about to unfold between her daughter and her husband any day now.

"Hello! Excuse Me," I interrupted, "There you go again."

She immediately brought her attention back to her breathing, and simply observed the flow, without trying to control it in any way.

"It's so amazing," she said after a while, "This breath that just keeps going in and out, in and out, on its own. If you think about it, it's the only thing that stands between life and death." She spent a few moments just marveling at this mystery, completely disregarding My role in the process.

Life is Death; Death is Life

Kaanja walked into his mother's room and planted a kiss on her forehead.

"How do you feel, Mom?" he asked, sitting down on the bed.

Kaanja's mother sat up in bed and took his hand in hers. "I'm feeling much better. What about you?"

"What's wrong with me?" Kaanja asked, knowing full well what she was referring to.

"You tell me," said his mother. "You were a bit harsh with your Dad yesterday, don't you think?"

"Don't worry, Mom. Dad's on his way up so we can talk." Kaanja got up from the bed and started pacing. "I think it's time we reach an agreement on my future and his expectations. I am not totally clear right now on what I want to do exactly, but I am totally clear that I don't want to take over Dad's business." Kaanja paused thoughtfully, for the first time actually finding some clarity on his ambition. "I know what you have gone through in life," he continued after a while, "And I can see a lot of lost opportunities for Kiara and her friends because they are girls. I want to somehow help change that in the world. I don't know if Dad will understand. Please help me to explain it to him."

"Just remember, Kaanja," his mother said softly, "Right or wrong, your Dad has lived his married life with only one goal: to give his family a better life. He is not looking for payback, but he is obviously concerned that everything he has built will just disappear."

"Mom, I have total faith in how this Universe operates. Dad has worked hard, worked honestly, and given to all of us unselfishly. The consequences of all this can never be negative for him. We just need to talk it through and find the solution that works for everyone."

At that moment, Kaanja's father walked into the room with a cup of tea for his wife.

"Kaanja wants to talk with us together," he said as he handed over the cup, "Are you feeling up to it?" he asked.

His wife took a deep breath and a sip of the hot tea, then gave her son a pleading look before saying, "Yes, I'm fine. I think it's high time we sort this out."

Kaanja immediately took the lead. "Look, Dad," he said with total honesty, "Before we get to me, I just want to say that I have tremendous respect for how you have lived your life and everything that you have done for us. Nothing that I say today should be interpreted to negate that fact."

Kaanja secretly instructed Me to be assertive if he started to lose his calm. He then went to his father, led him to a chair and asked him to sit down.

"Let's talk about you first," Kaanja said, suddenly wondering that while his father had done a great job of playing the supporting role in Kaanja's life story thus far, had Kaanja met his side of the agreement in playing the supporting role in his father's life story?

"When was the last time you actually did something for yourself, Dad? When was the last time you took a breather from your daily routine to assess if you are satisfied with where you are in your own life? Was this always your dream? To run a successful toy business?"

His father was visibly taken aback. "Dear Life!" he muttered under his breath.

"Yes, I am right here!" I blurted quickly before the moment could disappear.

He immediately connected. We went down memory lane together as he recalled his dream to become an author. He had lost his parents at a young age. There had been no choice but to start earning a living as soon as possible, which he had done by working at his uncle's fabric store. He had met Kaanja's mother when one day she had come to the store to buy some curtains.

He recalled all the objections he had faced from his uncle and aunt and the community when they found out that he had proposed to her. She was from a different culture, highly educated, and often came to the shop alone. The society was unforgiving, both to him and his wife. He had left his uncle's store and started making and selling small toys on the streets. Slowly, the business had grown enough to comfortably sustain his family. His wife had stood by him firmly through all the ups and downs in their life, but he was painfully aware of all the mental trauma she had suffered at the hands of the so-called society.

When Kiara was born, he had promised to himself that his daughter would never have to face anything like that. He would keep her safe.

By the time he had hit thirty, his dream of becoming an author had long been buried under the weight of his family responsibilities.

"If you were to do it all over again," I asked him, "Would you do anything differently?" Before I could even finish asking the question he was shaking his head sideways. "Everything that I did was to take care of my wife and children, and that's more important than anything else," he said.

The energy in the room became amazingly electric. The transformation was surreal! All three were connected to Me at the same time. It was like they were experiencing the Oneness of Me in real time, and no words were necessary to explain anything to each other. It was like I was experiencing Myself outside of a physical body! This is an extremely rare occurrence for Me where the purpose of my manifestations is served: To experience My own Oneness.

"Dad," Kaanja broke the silence softly, totally unaware himself of what he was about to say. "The whole purpose of life cannot be to just earn money and support a family. Each of us as an individual has a calling and so we are creating our life story with that purpose in mind, taking many detours with trials and errors. Our family and friends become our support system, so of course we need to nurture them, but they are a means to an end, not an end in itself. We are born, so inevitably we will die, but the life story will continue until the initial desire of each individual life story is fulfilled. It doesn't matter when we are born or when we will die; what matters is whether we covered the distance between life and death in a fulfilling manner."

Kaanja wondered if his Dad was understanding what he was trying to tell him. Kaanja had learnt to keep his spirituality to himself because he knew it made people uncomfortable if they were not operating at the same wavelength. He wondered if this would just make things awkward between him and his father from now on. His father had never been one to think beyond his immediate realities, but Kaanja really wanted his father to realize that there was more to reality than met the eye. It was a conversation he had thought about having with him many times, but the right opportunity had never really presented itself. This felt like the right time, and Kaanja wondered if this was how he was meant to support his father's life story.

Kaanja's father just stared at his son, totally speechless. He had always sensed that his son's understanding of Life and his wisdom were well beyond his limited years, but it suddenly felt like Kaanja had become the father. It was in that one fleeting moment that Kaanja's father understood Me as the common Life Force that is not constrained in any way by age, gender, race, or any other physical segregation that humanity has created.

"I think we as a family are lucky that we are all right Here, right Now, and in a position to support each other to get what each of us wants to get out of life," Kaanja continued. "It is time for you to play the lead role in your own life story and allow the rest of us to play the supporting role."

This was certainly not how Kaanja or his parents had imagined the discussion would go, but as soon as awareness starts to rise above the individual level, I am able to move forward in exactly what you would call the 'right' direction!

In Search of Life

Kiara walked into the room at that very moment, charged with an abundance of fighting energy.

She wondered if this is what self-realization felt like. All obstacles had quietly fallen away as soon as she accepted the fact that she and she alone was responsible and accountable for her life story. Everything she had experienced in life thus far was nothing more than the repercussions of her own choices and actions in the past. Enough was enough, she had decided. It was time that she stood up for herself!

She acknowledged that there was no way to change what she had already put in motion in terms of those repercussions, but realized that the only way to make sure future experiences would be in line with her desired life story was to start acting consciously from *now* onwards. She was determined to do exactly that, come what may. She had lived long enough in her head; it was time to live reality.

Kiara heard the last part of her brother's statement and froze in her tracks with surprise. Her father's life story? What life story? She had never really thought about that. What more could he want than to take care of his family? In that moment, she suddenly saw her father as an individual, who must have also had hopes and desires while he was growing up. Her father never really talked about his life before she and her brother were born. She knew his parents had died early, and she wondered now if he ever received the support that he would have needed to fulfill his own ambition.

Her father looked at her as she stood there, as if he was seeing her for the first time in his life. In a way, he was. It suddenly dawned on him that there was an independent life story at play right there; a life as respectable as his own, or his son's, or his wife's, or anyone else's in the world. It dawned on him that in his desire to keep her safe, he had unwittingly just perpetuated the societal norm that had rejected him and his wife. It dawned on him that every life has a right to live and experience life from the perspective of that particular physical body, irrespective of gender or any other categorization. He had given that right to his wife. He chided himself for having taken it away from his daughter.

He got up and hugged her. It wasn't the first time. One thing he had always lived with a total sense of fulfillment was his love for his family. He never held back when it came to expressing his love and appreciation. But this time, when he hugged her, it was with a new-found respect as his equal, and a new-found understanding of his responsibility to support her in *her* life story.

Kiara felt the difference. She stood there enjoying the moment. It was as if her total existence had compressed itself into this very moment. Life was right Here. Life was right Now.

She had come with a resolve to put her case in front of her father and fight it out to her last breath. But at this moment, she remembered nothing. She looked up at her father and wondered whether he was living his own life the way he had desired when he was her age.

Her father put his hands on her shoulders and shocked everyone by saying, "How would you like to start working for me as soon as school is over? Full-time for now, and part-time after college starts."

It was not like he wasn't aware of what his daughter was capable of, or what she wished she could do in life. He had seen her tampering with the toys many times and felt great pride at her intelligence. But he had been remiss in playing his supporting role in her life story, because he had misaligned himself with a social norm that he had rejected in his own life, somehow believing that it was the right way to protect his daughter. He realized now that protecting someone does not mean you take away the right of the person to make their own choices in life. His role was to provide guidance, and instill the values and skillsets which will enable her to make her own educated decisions, not to take the decisions on her behalf.

Kiara just stared at her father for what felt like an eternity. She then broke into tears in her father's arms and cried until no tears were left in her eyes. He let her; he knew there was a lot of pent-up resentment being released. He wondered how he had allowed it to accumulate to this level.

No-one felt the need to explain anything. It was as if their Life, not lives, was about to begin only *now*. It was as if everything they had experienced collectively throughout their existence had been leading up to this very moment, where everything just seemed to fall in place like pieces of a puzzle.

"Eight years," said her father as if there had been no interruption, "to get your MBA. After that, I will be writing my book full-time, and you will be managing the business any which way you want. Deal?"

"Deal!" screamed Kiara excitedly and gave her father another big hug. She ran over to her mother and gave her a hug too. Then she went over to Kaanja.

"Thank you," she said with a smile. She knew he had everything to do with their father's change of perspective.

"Don't thank me," said Kaanja as he gave her an affectionate hug, "I think we all just found Life."

"Hello, Excuse Me!" I said indignantly, "I was never lost; *you* all were. You have found *yourselves*. Welcome Home!"

I don't think anyone heard me because they were too busy absorbing the implications of what had just transpired.

The world outside continued to move forward exactly how it had been moving a moment ago, but Kaanja and his family's world had transformed miraculously.

Any onlooker would see Kaanja's mother sipping her second cup of tea in bed like before, but she is now thinking she needs to get another brand of tea because this one sucks!

Any onlooker would see Kaanja's father back at his desk sorting through his new toy blueprints like usual, but he is now sorting out the ones that he wants to run by his daughter, with a sense of joy and pride that he has never experienced before.

Any onlooker would see Kiara in her room reassembling a complicated toy for the umpteenth time, but she is now consumed with a sense of excitement and can no longer find any traces of what was only moments ago a deep-rooted frustration.

Any onlooker would see Kaanja lounging in his room on his bean bag, his ever-ready smile on his face. But he is now smiling because he no longer carries the heavy weight of the thought of one day having to disappoint his father.

All it took to change their world was a change in perspective. They all will go about their routine tomorrow in the same way as they had done today. But tomorrow, they will be consumed with a feeling of being exactly where they want to be in their lives. The ups and downs of experiences will continue, 'good' and 'bad' choices will continue to be made, but they will now feel more confident and ready to deal with whatever challenges show up at any moment because they are together, they are communicating, and they are taking life one experience at a time.

All because they answered my call, knowingly or unknowingly, even if only for a fleeting moment, and realized the value of being present, being connected, and using the current moment to renew themselves.

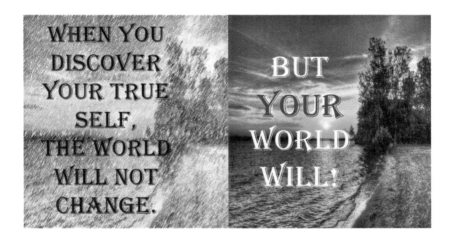

FIND YOURSELF; EVERYTHING ELSE IS ALREADY THERE

Life!

Kaanja counted thirty-five candles on his cake, wondering where the years had gone as he blew them out. His five-year old son could hardly contain himself as he immediately took a handful of the cake and smeared it all over his father's face with glee.

As his son tried to run away, Kaanja grabbed him by the waist and toppled his small face right into the cake on the table. His son screeched and laughed, then happily started licking the cake around his mouth.

Kaanja's mother shook her head and reached for a napkin. "Guess no one else will be having cake today," she said as she started to wipe off the cake from her grandson's face. She has continued to worry about her family over the years, but she has now gotten good at immediately catching her thoughts and transforming them into blessings.

At that moment, Kaanja's wife walked in with another cake in her hands. "Like I didn't know this was going to happen!" she chided, trying to act angry, but gave up when she took a look at her son's cake-smeared face. These are the moments life is made of, she thought happily, and I want to live every one of them fully!

Kaanja took a piece of cake to his father and sat down next to him. "I miss Kiara," he said, "This is the first time we are not celebrating our birthday together." Kiara still hasn't figured out how exactly she got the courage to make that bold move during her presentation seventeen years ago, and she doesn't really care. She has taken full control of her life and her choices. Her latest motivation is inventing eco-friendly toys that will be challenging and fun enough to lure kids away from their gaming consoles.

"Yes, I know," Kaanja's father smiled proudly, "Get used to celebrating your birthday without her. She will be travelling a lot now to manage the overseas branches!" Kaanja's father has not spoken to Me since that episode seventeen years ago, but he is really enjoying the time he spends on writing his book.

"How's your book coming along?" Kaanja asked.

"It's coming along," his father replied. "What is really challenging is that every time I think I have said what I feel is the right thing to say, something happens and my perspective changes. I am starting to think there's nothing one can say that will always remain true. Just the process of writing my thoughts down is so therapeutical, though. You are always saying life is about the journey, not the destination; well, I think I am finally beginning to understand what you mean! I may never finish the book, and that's fine."

As Kaanja lay in bed that night, he could not stop thinking about what his father had said. Is there anything indeed in this whole existence that forever remains constant, he wondered.

I decided not to interfere with his thought process. I wanted to see how far he had reached in his own evolution. Although he has always remained in constant touch with Me over the years, his passion for the advancement of girl education and empowerment in the world is where he spends a predominant amount of his energy. We are more in the texting mode these days than talking mode, hence I normally stay quiet when he spends many a night trying to solve the mysteries of the universe on his own before falling asleep.

Tonight, Kaanja focused his thoughts on the basic elements that are essential for life to survive, and wondered if these could be considered unchanging. He decided to put each of them through his logic test.

He started with Earth as the source of dust necessary for the formation of a physical body. Although one could take some of the dust and mold it into a vase and make it lose its identity to the vase, he thought, the dust nevertheless remains dust.

He then moved to water. Drops in the ocean are the ocean itself until a kid fills up a pale to build a sandcastle, at which point it gives the impression of being something different, but water remains water no matter what you mix it into.

The most irresistible example, he thought, is fire. Fire uses various mediums to manifest itself, but its essence always remains unchanged.

He also thought about space, abounding everywhere as one entity even though someone may constrain a part of it within four walls and a ceiling, and call it home instead.

And what about air, he mused? Air always flows freely as a single unit, even after we separate some by taking a breath and trapping some into our lungs.

He realized that while every essential element of life is actually a single entity, each could be made to experience separation from its source at the physical level through restriction or transformation. Perhaps that is the key to understanding the ultimate constant entity, he rationalized. Something that transforms when a finite piece is separated from It to become the earth or water or fire or space or air, yet remains unchanged in its essence. Perhaps It remains unchanged as the ultimate single source of energy for everything else, despite the experience of separations?

"How could you forget about Me," I finally intervened. "There's only One of Me, and I am the One that brings so many beings to life that look so different. I bring exactly the same characteristics to any living being I enter, although each uses them differently depending on the limitations of the physical apparatus. Even though I limit Myself within a physical apparatus, I remain unchanged in my Oneness, and continue to retain My full knowledge of Myself beyond the physical. I even retain My freedom to enter or leave a physical apparatus whenever I choose."

Kaanja was astonished, more with himself than with Me. "Of course!" he exclaimed, "Of course *you* are that *one* forever-constant entity that enables everything else to manifest!"

"I am like the sun that shines through the clouds as individual rays, until the clouds move along and reveal the one source behind what appeared to be individual streams of light," I continued. "In the same way, I shine through every physical apparatus, and My Oneness is revealed once the apparatus is removed."

For a long moment, Kaanja just rejoiced in that revelation. He tried to absorb the profoundness of the realization that, by logical deduction, he himself was One with everything and everyone else! He actually experienced it for just a moment in a way that he knew he would never be able to explain in words; that state of Just Being which creates endless ripples of illusions all around, yet remains totally untouched and unaffected by them.

"But *why*?" he asked finally, even though at some level he felt he knew the answer. "The question is *why* do You separate yourself into all this humungous, infinite activity?"

"If I am all there Is, then what else is there to do but for Me to experience Myself?" I asked. "I desire to experience the full potential of Myself. In every facet possible. I *know* that I am One, I must therefore create illusions of separation so I can *experience* My Oneness in all its glory, over and over again. Everything you experience as *you* is nothing more than an illusion of My separation from Myself."

Kaanja was unaware that he had fallen into a very deep sleep, while he continued the conversation with Me, or with Himself, in full awareness.

"We can all vouch for the fact that the most crucial aspect of our bodies is the ability to experience," he reasoned. "Physically, mentally, psychologically, spiritually. You name it. Any kind of experience we desire is possible, but only while we are in a physical apparatus."

"Exactly!" I responded. "Ultimately, the purpose of everything that exists is to enable that experience of Oneness. Each being must first experience the Oneness at the individual level. Whenever there is a critical mass shining through at the individual level, then the beings can actually experience My Oneness, or Their Oneness, at the collective level."

"But how to experience the Oneness at the individual level?" Kaanja asked. "There is so much noise all around us, so much variety, so much that only proves we are unique, separate and apart from everything and everyone else."

"Every manifestation is indeed unique," I confirmed, "because each one is instilled with the desire to create a unique experience. But when you recede into a state of just *being,* that is when you see the common thread that weaves together every manifestation. Just *be* the you that continues to be the same after changing name or religion. The you that continues to exist when arms and legs don't function. The you that continues to breathe when the heart pumping blood is made of silicon. The you that continues to *be* even when the brain is in a state of coma.

Just *be* the You that hides behind all the physical functioning and mental and social programming, behind all the experiences. Ground yourself in the You that simply observes all that is happening to the physical apparatus, in a neutral manner, without judging an experience as good or bad.

Recognize Me, the One Life Force that is flowing through you, through her, through him, through it; through anything and everything you perceive as a separate entity."

"But if all is One," insisted Kaanja, "then why is there so much hate and intolerance everywhere? Why would one part of You hate another part of You?"

I knew this was going to be our final conversation, because from now on, Kaanja was simply going to focus on making his choices every moment and savoring the resulting experiences. He had reached a stage in his awareness where it was impossible for Him to perceive a distinction between who was speaking, who was listening, and the knowledge itself. For him, all three aspects had merged into one.

"Why didn't you ask why there is so much love and compassion everywhere?" I asked. "For Me it's all the same; it's all an experience of My own potential. A physical apparatus charged by Me creates experiences based on its own choices, and then puts them into different categories. The truth is that experiencing light requires experiencing darkness as well, because otherwise it is not possible to differentiate between the two experiences. In the end, there is no gain, no loss; no life, no death; just continuous transformation of My energy.

Then Kaanja asked his final question.

"But where did *you* come from?"

"I came from nowhere, Kaanja, so I have nowhere to go. I am unborn, Kaanja, so I cannot die. And yes, Kaanja, when you die, I will still *be*. Ironically, what you experience as life, is a separation from Me; what you experience as death, is a reunion with Me.

When you leave the physical apparatus, you will realize that you thought you were a separate stream of the sunlight because of the clouds that were hiding the Truth. When the clouds clear, you will see that you never really went anywhere, because there is nowhere to go. You will always *be* right *here*, which encompasses Everywhere; you will always *be* right *now*, which encompasses Forever."

JUST BE